The
Touch of
Loneliness

Clark E. Moustakas is a faculty member of the Merrill-Palmer Institute in Detroit. He is also associated with other colleges and universities in workshops and seminars focusing on creativity and conformity, loneliness and individuality, child and family therapy, and human values and learning.

Dr. Moustakas is the author of *Loneliness, Loneliness and Love, Creativity and Conformity, Psychotherapy with Children, The Authentic Teacher, Portraits of Loneliness and Love, Finding Yourself, Finding Others,* and is co-author with Cereta Perry of *Learning to Be Free.*

The
Touch of
Loneliness

Clark E. Moustakas

Prentice-Hall, Inc.   Englewood Cliffs, New Jersey

Library of Congress Cataloging in Publication Data

MOUSTAKAS, CLARK E
 The touch of loneliness.

 1. Loneliness—Addresses, essays, lectures.
 2. Moustakas, Clark E. Loneliness. I. Title.
 BF575.L7M67   158'.2   74-34191
 ISBN 0-13-924696-7
 ISBN 0-13-924688-6 pbk.

©1975 by CLARK E. MOUSTAKAS
ENGLEWOOD CLIFFS, NEW JERSEY

A SPECTRUM BOOK

10 9 8 7 6 5 4 3 2 1

Printed in the United States of America

PRENTICE-HALL INTERNATIONAL, INC. *(London)*
PRENTICE-HALL OF AUSTRALIA PTY., LTD. *(Sydney)*
PRENTICE-HALL OF CANADA, LTD. *(Toronto)*
PRENTICE-HALL OF INDIA PRIVATE LIMITED *(New Delhi)*
PRENTICE-HALL OF JAPAN, INC. *(Tokyo)*

Acknowledgments

Being involved in *The Touch of Loneliness* took me to many significant times in the past that are still alive within me. I want to express in this way my valuing of the letters from the persons who shared their response to my book *Loneliness* and went on to convey something of the impact of the lonely process in their own lives. I express my appreciation to the following persons for their permission to include in this book what they have written in lonely times.

Helen DeRosis (pp. 36–37), Ann Stone (pp. 40–42), Bonnie M. Hawkes (p. 43), Harold Lyon, Jr. (pp. 46–47)—also in modified form in *It's Me and I'm Here!* (Delacorte Press, 1974), Arleen Rainis (p. 50), Pariskevi Kalodimas (pp. 41–44), Alma Stone (p. 61) from "Remember Me to Life," *Psychiatry* (1974) 37:158–170, p. 170, Bennie White (p. 62), Linda Shakleton (pp. 72–73), Sylvia Tansey (p. 76), Barbara Mazie (pp. 80–81), Laurene Krispin (p. 82), Jerry Williams (pp. 83–84), Ross Mooney (p. 86) and Laura Newman (pp. 89–90). I also thank the many persons whom I was unable to reach or who preferred to remain anonymous.

Becky Naghaski was particularly helpful in meeting critical deadlines, and Mavis Wolfe stayed with me in the final typing of the manuscript.

I also want to speak positively to the many persons here at Merrill-Palmer, in Detroit, and in colleges and universities throughout the country who have been receptive and affirming in opening the process of self-discovery that comes through loneliness and who have been willing to portray these experiences in verbal communication, in letters, diaries, poems, stories, and in art, music, and dance forms.

For Bob and Nancy Moustakas

You trust the organic flow of life
the magic in plants and trees
and elemental things
In simple ways you touch
what is essential
in yourself and others

Contents

The
Touch of
Loneliness

I
The Loneliness
Each Man Feels
Is His Hunger for Life

Several months ago, I was asked to write a preface for a new hardcover edition of my book *Loneliness*. Although the preface was never written, it started me on a totally unexpected journey—a return to letters and papers of loneliness that I wrote to myself in times of challenge, crisis, and tragedy, and letters of other people, describing their struggles with loneliness, their fears of self-discovery, and the often painful process of choosing life over death.

For many years now, my writing has been an essential form of self-expression, a way of coming to terms with issues and problems of living. Since my writing grows out of an inner need, it is often a basic resource of self-awareness that leads to important changes in my work and in my relations. Rarely have I chosen to write as a response to another's request or invitation. Either the process begins through inner necessity or it doesn't.

Thus, this new venture into loneliness has developed from my own excitement, determination, and thrust to create.

I have been thinking of the way my life has changed since the publication of *Loneliness*. Over these years, I have traveled throughout the United States offering workshops on loneliness as it relates to solitude, alienation, crisis, creativity, communication, and relationships. One of these workshops at Esalen Institute turned into an encounter group and opened an entirely different way of working with people. For awhile this represented an extreme change, involving a dominant core of participation, and I began substituting direct, active confrontation for the simple, compassionate ways that formally had characterized my relationships with others. That extreme shift was eventually modified when I came to my senses, back to my own roots, where sensitivity and tenderness, a valuing of gradual unfolding of life, and respect for each person's timetable were once more embraced as cornerstones of my philosophy of human relations.

College students and other young people especially responded to the alienation that surrounded them, the emptiness and impersonal ways of life. Quickly they saw loneliness as a way back to themselves. It represented an opportunity for awareness and new life, and a challenge to tell their stories creatively through music, art, and poetry. Often, there was such a strong response, such a release and opening in these young people, that what started as an hour's presentation lasted through late hours of the night. *Loneliness* represented a breakthrough for many young people who for the first time directly faced the reality of separateness and the agony of a process that often brought fear, pain and isolation. Many of these people wept openly and freely in the realization of the solitary nature of crucial experience and crisis, and many chose loneliness to deal with significant questions and problems and to find a new path of being that would respect privacy and individuality and that would lead to new ways of being and relating.

As a result of my studies, I began to view children in school settings and in therapy from a different perspective. I no longer saw withdrawal as an automatic danger but began to relate to the actual meaning of silence and solitude for a specific child. Often, it became clear that isolated activity was not a problem for the child, as teachers and parents often claimed. Rather it was a particular way of being, a way of responding to inner life, a satisfying process that expressed itself in fantasy, imagination, day dreaming, and meditation. Through my understanding of the significance of these solitary sources of life, I have been able to assist teachers and parents to respect the quiet presence of a child engaged in creations of the self. This has resulted in a series of classroom experiments utilizing the arts and humanities as ways of enriching and humanizing learning and as ways of fostering and encouraging individuality, autonomy, and self-direction.

In a number of hospitals an entirely new attitude arose in response to children's cries against separation from parents and their fears of facing unknown terrors entirely alone. Visiting hours have been extended in many hospitals and parents have been invited, even encouraged to remain with their child through the process of surgery and major illness. Workshops with nurses and physicians in hospitals and university training programs revealed that some medical professionals were beginning to view a child's protest and rebellion in hospitals as a natural response to his or her being deprived of contact with family members. At no time is the support of loving relations more important than during a crisis, and this is particularly crucial for a young child facing the unknown of disease and surgery and the terror and pain connected with hospital tests, instruments and procedures. More and more hospital workers are realizing that the indifference, depression, and anomie of the hospital child are often far more serious than the physical breakdown of cells, tissues, and organs. The child's strengths are energized through the caring support of hospital personnel, and the continuing love of family and friends. Many mothers and some fathers wrote that *Loneliness* gave them the courage to take a stand in hospitals where the administration's hostile and impersonal attitudes tried to push them away and frighten them into abandoning their child.

Another avenue of communication, in addition to workshops, was through correspondence with people who were touched by *Loneliness*. Letters, poetry, stories, and other art forms opened a series of exchanges resulting in friendships that have enriched my life. It was of tremendous value to learn about the impact of loneliness in other people's lives, its positive powers, and its use in coming to grips with tragedy. For many people, shame was eliminated once loneliness was felt and owned.

The creation of *Loneliness* had a significant impact in terms of my own self, my self-awareness, and the realization that loneliness is a basic ingredient of my being. When I openly recognized myself as a lonely person, this awareness and acceptance enabled me to live with critical moments, manipulation, deceit, and betrayal. Through a recognition of my own solitude and periods of isolation, I have been able to continue to live on the basis of ethical and moral values. Loneliness has helped me stay up when everything else in my world seemed to be going down. I no longer need to find substitutes or search for explanations or causes but can depend upon my own realizations and discoveries to point the way.

Loneliness spoke for me. Colleagues, family and friends understood and supported my pilgrimages, viewed my lonely journeys as natural, as characteristic of me. Though I am certain it has sometimes been painful for others to permit me to wander away alone when I was plagued by a problem or living with shattered moments, tragedies, and broken communications, most people respected my solitude and saw it as my way of communion with myself and not as a rejection of them or an indication of loss or absence. Going off alone in prolonged isolation became my way to self-renewal, awakening optimism and hope, and returning to a fuller life with others. All the major shifts in my work with people, my growth in self-awareness, and the significant choices I have made have come through solitary struggles, poems, songs, stories, tears and laughter, and the embracing of life. Everything of significance expressed in *Loneliness* has borne fruit in my own life and continues to be the central source of self-growth and growth in my relations with others.

I shall mention one specific example of self-growth that came through loneliness. It seems evident as I write now, but the understanding and change came through a lengthy process of struggling and searching to find a new way to be with others who were suffering, especially people in the critical stages of terminal illness. For many years, when I was with critically ill persons I experienced their pain as my own. Although I could clearly see that this often plunged the person into a greater agony, I seemed unable to transcend my own response. At times the other person did not want to focus on their own pain, but my facial and body expression often intensified and increased the other's anguish. The pain of the finality of the illness and the suffering was so strongly present that we became deeply immersed in death rather than creating and maintaining whatever life was still available to us. I discovered that if I went off alone with my own anguish before my visit, in some miraculous way I could approach the critically ill person with a thrust toward creating life. The pain was still there within me but it was no longer central. Instead I felt an inner tranquility and a readiness for conversation, simple activity, or even silence. I was able to share what there is of life rather than dwelling in the darkness of death and dying. The other person may still choose to stay with the pain or terror but I no longer add to that suffering; in some ways I believe my positive human presence gives strength to the other person to face the ending and the unknown. I have learned, at last, simply to be with a lonely person in the full human sense. Often that is all that is needed to help the person face a crisis, become aware of feelings, see new directions, and take the active steps needed to change or live with tragedy. Loneliness calls for a human presence whose power is silent, invisible, indescribable. Though it is sometimes painful to be recognized in the deep reaches of one's self, it can be a completely beautiful and freeing experience.

The influence and impact of loneliness as it touches the lives of people in many different human situations is recounted in the letters that people have shared with me. Each of these tell of crucial moments when loneliness was the breakthrough to new hope. As I searched into my records of the past 12 years I also came across many letters that I had written to myself and others, illustrating my own use of the loneliness process as a significant resource for growth. I believe that these letters and papers offer a new vision of the touch of loneliness and the growing realization of its essential contribution to human sensibilities and human activities. Through loneliness a level of honesty is reached that brings character and substance into a person's life.

In the midst of my journey back in time with people who have supported my discoveries and enriched my life, I received a letter from my friend, Dorothy Lee, that moved me forward in the creation of this book. "What a beautiful, moving collection of letters. I want to urge you to publish them. They are part of your theme of loneliness—what was evoked by your own discovery and suffering, by your deepening feeling and thinking. Everything you have written before and after is subsumed—oh what a word!—is and always was the base and substance of your awareness of loneliness, the purity of self, the pain of realization, the sheer pain of unverted, unpadded self, and the base of relatedness, the torture, too, of not-being-able-to-be or relate, alien for yourself, the strangling tree, the breeze, the rock, your neighbor. Loneliness is to me the miracle of unadulterated, unopaque *me,* the exquisite pain and glory of *me.*"

Ross Mooney offered this strong affirmation of loneliness as a way of creating life:

> The loneliness each man feels is his hunger for life itself, not only life in his being, but life in the being of creation, past, present and future. Your book *Loneliness* allows the reader to recognize his own vacuum which is the first step to appreciation of its filling. Had you left your own vacuum uncomposed in expression, you would have left others with nothing (a disparate emptiness); composing it, you gave others not only a chance of recognizing their own, but also a way of composing a view of one's emptiness as one visualizes the cup in a ring, inviting the placement of the pearl of great price. It is the yearning that makes fulfillment possible in the most elemental ranges. It is death present within life, without which there could not be life.

2
Loneliness—
Unraveling Its Power
and Meaning

My interest in loneliness began at a critical time in my life when I was faced with the problem of whether or not to agree to major heart surgery that might restore my daughter to health or result in her death. I did not consciously set out to study loneliness. I had no research design or hypotheses or assumptions. The urgency of making a critical decision plunged me into the experience of feeling utterly alone, and pushed me to deliberately cut myself off from the advice or guidance of others. The entire process of facing the terror and potential consequence of this life or death decision initiated a search into my own self, an engagement of disturbing inner contact in which I tried to be fully aware and discover the right way to proceed. The probing increased my sense of isolation and took me on many lonely paths, each of which ended in a question mark.

Lonely self-reflection came at unexpected moments, in the midst of a crowd of people, in response to a word or phrase in conversation. Many different kinds of situations evoked an inner process of doubt and uncertainty, and a strong feeling of being alone. Sometimes I awakened in the night, overwhelmed by images and feelings and thoughts. I tried to draw from myself a single answer that would utilize the significant data that came from conversations with my daughter, talks with physicians, and published reports on heart surgery. Thus, the initial journey into loneliness was an attempt to discover the one true way to proceed: it involved a process of self-inquiry, which was not planned but simply happened, was not carefully sampled but occurring spontaneously at unexpected times and places. Although no answer came to the problem of surgery, I became aware that at the center of my world was a deep and pervasive feeling of loneliness. With this feeling came the realization that loneliness is a capacity or source in man for new searching, awareness, and inspiration—that when the outside world ceases to have a meaning, when support and confirmation are lacking or are not adequate to assuage human suffering, when doubt and uncertainty overwhelm a person, then the individual may contemplate life from the depths of his own self and in nature. For me, this discovery meant that in a crucial and compelling crisis, in spite of comfort and sympathy from others, one can feel utterly and completely alone, that, at bottom, the experience of loneliness exists in its own right as a source of power and creativity, as a source of insight and direction. I saw loneliness as a require-ment of living no matter how much love and affirmation one receives in work and in relationships with others.

Thus, the beginning steps of my research—unconscious research at first—into loneliness involved not a question of the *nature* of loneliness, or its restorative, creative, or destructive impact on the person, but a struggle and search into *another* problem. Much later I realized that loneliness is often experienced by individuals who make crucial decisions that will have major consequences in the lives of others. Through inner exploration and study, I sought to find a solution that would integrate the facts into one clear pattern. The signifi-cance of inner searching for deeper awareness is cogently expressed by Michael Polanyi in his book *Science, Faith and Society*:

> Every interpretation of nature, whether scientific, non-scientific or
> anti-scientific, is based on some intuitive conception of the general nature

of things. . . . But in spite of much beautiful work . . . we still have no clear conception of how discovery comes about. The main difficulty has been pointed out by Plato in the *Meno*. He says that to search for the solution of a problem is an absurdity. For either you know what you are looking for, and then there is no problem; or you do not know what you are looking for, and then you are not looking for anything and cannot expect to find anything. . . . A potential discovery may be thought to attract the mind which will reveal it—inflaming the scientist with creative desire and imparting to him intimations that guide him from clue to clue and from surmise to surmise. The testing hand, the straining eye, the ransacked brain, may all be thought to be labouring under the common spell of a potential discovery striving to emerge into actuality.

Experiences in meditation and self-searching, intuitive and mystical reachings, and hours of silent midnight walking paved the way to a formulation of my understanding of loneliness; this formulation emerged clearly during my observations of hospitalized children./In the hospital I saw how lonely feelings impelled young children to seek a compassionate voice and a warm, friendly face; I saw how young children separated from their parents could often be more completely involved in the struggle with loneliness than in the painful experiences connected with illness and surgery; I observed how these children underwent a period of protest and resistance against separation, against the mechanical actions and fixed faces and gestures of the hospital combine. I also observed a gradual deterioration of protest, rebellion, and self-assertion to be replaced by a deep sense of isolation, lonely weeping, withdrawal, depression, and numbness. In general, I witnessed a basic, pervasive feeling of dehumanization, an institution that not only sought to repress lonely feelings but discouraged the whole range of human emotions that characterize the alive and growing child.

When I saw that these dimensions of loneliness were almost totally ignored, misunderstood, and misinterpreted by hospital aides, nurses, and doctors, I decided, using the hospital situation and my own intuitive awareness as a beginning, to study the nature of loneliness, how it fitted into the perceptions and behavior of hospitalized children, and the way in which it existed in myself and others. I decided to listen to the experiences of children in the hospital, without taking notes and making records, but keeping the focus of my interest on the essence of the lonely experience through the person's rendering of it. I wanted to know the truth of the lonely process in its most basic, objective forms.

Objectivity, in this connection, means seeing what an experience *is* for another person—not its cause, its reason for existence, nor its definition and classification. It means seeing attitudes, beliefs, and feelings of the person as they exist at the moment, perceiving them whole, as a unity. I set out to know the meaning of loneliness, not by defining and categorizing, but by experiencing it directly myself and through the lives of others, as a simple reality of life as George E. Moore describes reality in *Principia Ethica*:

> My point is that "good" is a simple notion, just as "yellow" is a simple notion; that, just as you cannot, by any manner of means, explain to any one who does not already know it, what yellow is, so you cannot explain what good is. Definitions of the kind that I was asking for, definitions which describe the real nature of the object or notion denoted by a word, and which do not merely tell us what the word is used to mean, are only possible when the object or notion in question is something complex. You can give a definition of a horse, because a horse has many different properties and qualities, all of which you can enumerate. But when you have enumerated them all, when you have reduced a horse to his simplest terms, then you can no longer define those terms. They are simply something which you think of or perceive, and to any one who cannot think of or perceive them, you can never, by any definition, make their nature known.

I set out to discover the meaning of loneliness in its simplest terms and in its native state. I knew from my own experiences and from my conversations with hospitalized children that loneliness itself could not be communicated by words or defined in its essence, or appreciated and recognized except by persons who are open to their own senses and aware of their own experiences. I set out to discover the nature of lonely experience by intimate encounter with other persons. A quotation from Polanyi's *Personal Knowledge* will clarify this point:

> To say that the discovery of objective truth in science consists in the apprehension of a rationality which commands our respect and arouses our contemplative admiration; that such discovery, while using the experience of our senses as clues, transcends this experience by embracing the vision of a reality beyond the impression of our senses, a vision which speaks for itself in guiding us to an ever deeper understanding of reality—such an account of scientific procedure would be generally shrugged aside as out-dated Platonism; a piece of mystery-mongering unworthy of an enlightened age. Yet it is precisely on this conception of objectivity that I wish to insist. . . . Into every act of knowing there enters a passionate contribution of the person knowing what is known, and . . . this coefficient is no mere imperfection but a vital component of his knowledge.

Initially, I studied loneliness in its essential forms, by putting myself into an open, ready state, into the lonely experiences of hospitalized children, letting these experiences become the focus of my world. I listened. I watched. I stood by. In dialogue with the child, I tried to put into words the depth of his or her feelings. Sometimes my words touched the child and tears began to flow; sometimes the child formed words in response to my presence, and broke through the numbness and the dehumanizing impact of the hospital atmosphere and practice. In a strong sense, loneliness became my existence. It entered into every facet of my world—into my teaching, my interviews in therapy, my conversations with friends, my home life. Without reference to time or place or structure, somehow (more intentionally than accidentally) the loneliness theme came up everywhere in my life. At this time, I became clearly aware that, exhaustively and fully, and in a caring way, I was searching for, studying, and inquiring into the nature and impact of loneliness. I was totally immersed in the search for a pattern that would reveal the various dimensions of loneliness. This was research in the sense of a close searching and inquiring into the nature of a human experience and not from a detached intellectual or academic viewpoint. Rather, my studies involved an integrative, living form; I became part of the lonely experiences of others, involved and interested, while at the same time aware of an emerging pattern. Facts and knowledge accumulated as I listened and later recorded and studied them; but, at the same time, there were intuitive visions, feelings, and sensings that went beyond anything I could record or know in a factual sense. At the center of each lonely existence were ineffable, indescribable feelings and experiences, which I felt in a unified and essential way. I had, at moments, gone "wide open," ceasing to be a separate individual, but wholly related to the other person, leaving something behind of my own intuitive vision, and comprehension while, at the same time, taking something away—very much in the manner that John Steinbeck and Edward F. Ricketts approached their study of the *Sea of Cortez*:

> Let's see what we see, record what we find, and not fool ourselves with conventional scientific strictures—in that lonely and uninhabited Gulf our boat and ourselves would change it the moment we entered. By going there, we would bring a new factor to the Gulf. Let us consider that factor and not be betrayed by this myth of permanent objective reality. If it exists at all it is only available in pickled tatters or in distorted flashes. "Let us go," we said, "into the Sea of Cortez, realizing that we become

forever a part of it; that our rubber boots slogging through a flat of eelgrass, that the rocks we turn over in a tide pool, make us truly and permanently a factor in the ecology of the region. We shall take something away from it, but we shall leave something too." And if we seem a small factor in a huge pattern, nevertheless it is of relative importance. We take a tiny colony of soft corals from a rock in a little water world. And that isn't terribly important to the tide pool. Fifty miles away the Japanese shrimp boats are dredging with overlapping scoops, bringing up tons of shrimps, rapidly destroying the ecological balance of the whole region. That isn't very important in the world. And six thousand miles away the great bombs are falling on London and the stars are not moved thereby. None of it is important or all of it is.

Thus, I began a formal study of loneliness, combining my own growing self-awareness and the discovery of myself as a lonely person with my experiences in the hospital, and conversations and discussions with other persons—children in school settings, who spoke freely and openly and wrote themes expressing their lonely experiences; parents and young adults in therapy, who initially found it painful to speak of loneliness but were soon able to recapture and create in a living sense moments of the past and current feelings of isolation and solitude; and friends and colleagues, who revealed in intimate terms the impact of the loneliness experience. I steeped myself in a world of loneliness, letting my life take root and unfold in it, letting its dimensions and meanings and forms evolve in its own timetable and dynamics and ways.

The study culminated in my readings of published reports on loneliness and lonely experiences. But this was a point near the end, not at the beginning, where it might have acted to predispose and predetermine and color my own growing awareness. I studied biographies and autobiographies of individuals who dramatically exemplified lonely lives: Emily Dickinson, Abraham Lincoln, Woodrow Wilson, Benedict Arnold, and Ned Langford. I followed the lonely experiences

Buhl in his journey to the highest peak of the
Admiral Byrd alone on an advanced base in
Saint Exupéry lost in the desert, and other persons
extreme situations of isolation. To understand
more fully the lonely consequences of infamy and mass public
rejection, I studied the autobiographical volumes of Alger Hiss
and Whitaker Chambers as well as political analyses of their
trial and its implications, including the volumes of the House
Unamerican Activities Committee and the ten volumes of the
trial transcript. I discovered additional nuances of the meaning of loneliness from the studies of Frieda Fromm-Reichmann
of the loneliness of mental patients, Margaret Wood's *Paths of
Loneliness*, Eithne Tabor's *Songs of a Psychotic*, Karl Menninger's
Love Against Hate, David Riesman's *The Lonely Crowd*, Erich
Fromm's *Escape from Freedom*, Thomas Wolfe's *Hills Beyond*,
Sullivan's *Interpersonal Theory of Psychiatry*. The numerous arti-
cles and reports appearing in newspapers and journals also
received my attention; these accounts could be interpreted as
attempts to overcome loneliness and as evolutions of deeper
sensitivity and awareness that enabled unique and creative
expressions of loneliness in poetry, music, literature, and other
art forms.

When a pattern began to emerge with reference to the
nature and function of loneliness in individual experience and
in modern living, the formal study came to an end. At this
point the framework and the clarification of loneliness had
been formed; it was possible to differentiate and refine its
meaning, to expand and illustrate its nature and relevance in
human experience. Thus what started as a hospital study of
loneliness became an extended search into the phenomenon of
loneliness.

The chain of conditions and factors that initiated and
characterized the study were as follows: (1) a crisis, which

created a question or problem; (2) a search of self in solitude, from which emerged a recognition of the significance of loneliness both as a creative urging and as a frightening and disturbing experience; (3) an expanding awareness through being open to lonely life and lonely experiences, through watching, listening, and feeling and through conversation, dialogue, and discussion; (4) a steeping of myself in the deeper regions of loneliness, so that it became the center of my world; (5) an intuitive grasping of the patterns of loneliness, and related aspects and different associations, until an integrated vision and awareness emerged; (6) further clarification, delineation, and refinement through studies of lonely lives, lonely experiences, and published reports on loneliness; and (7) creation of a manuscript in which to project and express the various forms, themes, and values of loneliness and to present its creative powers, as well as the anxiety it arouses in discontent, restlessness, and boredom, and the strategies used in attempting to overcome and escape loneliness.

My studies awakened me to the creative power of loneliness, and the values it offers in the process of searching and studying. I saw the value of being open to significant dimensions of experience in which comprehension and compassion mingle; intellect, emotion, and spirit are integrated; and intuition, spontaneity, and self-exploration are seen as components of unified experience. Discovery and creation are reflections of a serious search into human ventures, processes, and experiences.

Since the publication of *Loneliness*, I have received approximately 1,000 letters that validate my portrayal of the nature of loneliness in modern life. My correspondents confirmed the meaning and essence of loneliness that had emerged from my research; each of these persons portrayed the uniqueness of lonely experience and its powers in drawing upon untouched capacities and resources, in evolving new creations, and expanding awareness, sensitivity, and compassion. They revealed also the extreme pain, grief, despair, and impotency that often accompany the urge to discover, and answer the challenges and problems of living. I have selected a number of these letters that awaken significant dialogue between myself and others. They represent an opportunity for readers to talk back to an author, to say for themselves how loneliness touched their lives, and what it expresses in the way of creation. The fear of self-discovery is a strong component in avoiding loneliness and solitude. Once this courageous step is taken, however, there is no turning back, as these letters attest.

References

MOORE, GEORGE E. *Principia Ethica*. New York and London: Cambridge University Press, Paperback edition; 1959.

MOUSTAKAS, CLARK. *Loneliness*. Englewood Cliffs, N. J.: Prentice-Hall, 1961.

POLANYI, MICHAEL. *Personal Knowledge*. Chicago: University of Chicago Press, 1958.

POLANYI, MICHAEL. *Science, Faith and Society*. First Phoenix edition. Chicago: University of Chicago Press, 1964.

ROGERS, CARL R. "Some Thoughts Regarding the Current Philosophy of the Behavioral Sciences." Unpublished paper. La Jolla, Calif.: Western Behavioral Sciences Institute, 1964.

STEINBECK, JOHN, and RICKETTS, EDWARD F. *Sea of Cortez*. New York: Viking Press, 1941.

3
Loneliness and Self–Discovery:
Letters to Myself
—from Others

"In loneliness I have my own dream"

I am writing you as, perhaps, many others have, upon reading your book on loneliness. It was difficult for me to muster up the courage to lift the cover and enter a world that I feared would tell me what I didn't want to know.

In vain I've tried to build bridges. Despondent, confused, with no other alternative than panic and suicide I would commit myself to the prison-like cacophony and discord of a mental institution.

Loneliness . . . the word has always brought with it an air of apartness, as one removed from throbbing, pulsing day-to-day paces.

How can I tell you? Today in spite of all my need to love and be loved, I still prefer moments of relief . . . alone. I'm soft and pliable clay, but I, too, have my own dreams.

It is odd how I feared reading your book—dreaded finding myself there in among the pages—oh, the name is different and perhaps the age but too much is a part of *me*. The "me" no one knows, so deep, so buried that it only comes out in a peaceful moment, alone. In the peaceful moment I am free, free of pressure or panic. Deep, vibrant warm, calm, enveloping a beauty that is trampled in the madness of *here* and *now*. Aloft, without vanity or smugness are tears of joy. Only then have I felt the peace and depth of my real self. The days are filled with the struggle for survival, the nights often tense, full of the day's anxieties.

Who I am I have scarcely begun to know. Living in the shadow of fear and mockery from a tyrannical parent (father), pushed about with more mockery in mental institutions, I escaped reality by fantasies filled with gentleness and love, something I had never found enough of in my real world. Perhaps it is the hungry need to be alone, somewhere, if only for a peaceful moment.

"Dance a story"

Rather than making solitude an act of discovery many people are so busy manipulating and imposing that they have lost touch with themselves and therefore with the real world. This is often true of teachers and counselors who fail to take the time to be alone and discover what really matters in life.

For four years now, I have been involved in a major effort to bring human values to life in the classroom. In this connection, as I sit alone here by the seashore, I am recalling my brief encounter with Lisa. Wide awake and alert to sources of life, Lisa taught me how quickly a child sometimes learns in contrast to the prolonged struggle adults experience.

I met Lisa on one of my western trips. She and her father had met me at the airport. On the way to my motel, Lisa engaged me in conversation. In her opening remark she expressed her hatred of school, especially of being forced to read "dumb pages and answer dumb questions from a dumb book." She described her dream of a school where learning was enjoyable and where reading was your own thing. I wondered whether her father had coached her, for almost immediately she asked about my work. I had just had an exciting time with a group of second graders so I decided to share my experience with her. I related how children developed an organic vocabulary by using their own special words in reading, writing, and speech. I described our project of the previous day—"Dance a Story." Silently children created imaginative stories with their own favorite words. Then, in their dances, children portrayed feelings of loneliness, anger, joy, fear, and problems in their relations with parents, teachers, and friends. They selected their own piece of music and pantomimed and danced their own stories. Some of these children wrote their stories afterwards and put them in their portfolios of special creations.

Lisa listened with rapt attention but remained absolutely quiet the rest of the trip. The next morning her father arrived for my workshop. He opened the session by sharing the events of the previous evening with the entire group. When they reached home, Lisa led her father to the living room and told him she had something she wanted to share with him. She carefully selected a record album and proceeded to dance her story. The dance depicted her suffering and loneliness, scenes that portrayed the loss of her mother. Until that moment she had not communicated with anyone the impact of her mother's death. Lisa ended her dance story with tears and rushed to embrace her father. She told him that she loved him and that she was glad he was alive. Then they talked together, openly and freely, for the first time since the death of Lisa's mother.

The value of movement and music in children's learning is not a rare experience but Lisa's ingenious way of using the "Dance a Story" affirmed my belief that children need options and creative alternatives that will evoke inner feelings when the moment is right. Through this dance form Lisa was able to share her loneliness, experience a release, and deepen the bond with her father. Her experience inspired me to keep on urging the creation of human classrooms.

C.M.

"I can live another day"

I received your letter, which warmed my heart and filled me with a glow of warmth and happiness; as yours was the first personal letter I've received in months. I have wanted to write you many times myself, as much as I felt some life still within me, instead of pains in my chest or the flu or pneumonia or grief. You're right, really; it makes no difference that there is pain and suffering and ugliness, as long as both in nature and in any human relationship a little warmth, a definite caring exists and grows; as long as a person can say to himself and feel in relation to another, that caring and loving are always present, even in the most unbearable situations; and as long as bitterness, self-pity and hurt do not ride fully the reins of a human heart.

What makes me so depressed, or suffer and ache, I don't know—I know sometimes I feel on the verge of suicide, and each time I have reached the actual crisis and am ready to carry through, morning comes or a face smiles or a color or shape or scene warms my heart, such as your letter today; and within I say do not kill yourself, wait, live, and I don't feel so depressed and don't kill myself, and by a hair, as if by the grace of God, I can live another day, and with all my heart I am grateful to be spared such a tragic ending—what hurts is that I can only keep going and have lost almost my power to give and share and create and am only able to hang on a little more—maybe this is why at times a rainbow may not exist, yet we all know it does if one looks around him where he is rather than where he thinks he should be.

I remember vividly when my family left me I missed them terribly. I tried to go to church to take part in the New Year's service. I had had a little wine plus feeling sick all over. During the service I sat, waited for my turn to read the Scriptures. I got up to take my place at the lectern—it took all the effort, all the energy and courage I could have mustered. I turned to the page, took a glance around the congregation and all at once I broke down and had to leave the church—I fell apart like a house built of toothpicks when I got outside. I waited for a bus, my heart pounding. I felt as if I had been dropped from a twenty-story building and tears rolled and everything became dark—I have felt that way ever since— becoming more depressed—physically more sick—pulled through double pneumonia but haven't been at my best—only for very, very short periods—sometimes it seems as if for only a few breaths and then weeks and weeks of gloom.

You may wonder what is the most valuable thing in my life. In thinking this through, there is only one answer—a friend- ship that began with *Loneliness*.

"Using a pickaxe to no purpose makes a prison"

I have rediscovered after 12 years your book published in 1961, *Loneliness*. It meant a lot to me in 1962 when my husband and I were living in New Mexico. But today, in 1974, when a very stark loneliness suddenly confronted me, I was overwhelmed by its profound meaning and message.

Although my husband and I were particularly involved with American Indian peoples in the last years of his life, since his death in 1968 I have become profoundly involved in other minority group affairs as well, particularly those minority-group individuals who are prison inmates. The quote on p. 60 of *Loneliness* from St. Exupéry is particularly significant for prison inmates: "Prison is not a mere physical horror. It is using a pickaxe to no purpose that makes a prison; the horror resides in the failure to enlist all those who swing the pick in the community of mankind."

I have wondered whether you or any of your students or associates have considered or indeed are already involved in making the experience of loneliness, especially for prisoners in solitary confinement for long periods, a meaningful experience of personal inner growth, enlargement of mental and spiritual horizons, and the discovery that limitations such as cement walls, iron bars, hostile "keepers," and isolation can indeed be the challenge to discover the richness of the world within?

If no one in your knowledge has as yet considered this kind of contribution may I suggest it as a most terribly needed one?

"Snap drugs straight out of my mind"

I really don't know how to start this letter, but right now I am incarcerated and in the process of rehabilitating myself from drug addiction. You see I want 100 percent to snap drugs straight out of my mind. I know it's going to be a hard job doing it, but I think through loneliness I finally found my real self in here, and this is why I think when I am released from here, I won't need drugs anymore to keep me going—if I do I'll be a fool, [because] I think anyone who takes drugs needs guidance and really to find his self before it is too late; and I also found out that everybody is better than what they think they are. They could do it if they really want to. All it takes is a little understanding in one's self and willpower and also guidance to lead such a person to take a good look at his self, and ask his self does he really need these drugs to get where he wants to be? I don't think so!

"Knowing our own touchings of the other"

I have just read your book, *Loneliness*. How it recalls, not many to be sure, but several searing experiences in my life, to which you have set words. My impulse is to say—which you have set to music with your inner revelations, because of the beauty and grandeur of music. Yet, perhaps none compares with the staggering impact of the experiences of which you speak.

These times have occurred, as you say, at the times of childbirth, at a child's illness, at the moment of decision concerning one's belief, or lack of it, in the divine. And then more frequently, with similar impact strangely enough, yet with less intensity, during the "little" moments of our exist-ence—knowing, for a fleeting moment, that differences exist without the need for making comparisons, knowing our own touchings of the other. All this we can only know alone. Some of us can express them, as you have, some of us keep them locked in our hearts. And this is even more painful, because it is only with the occasional comings out of our loneliness that we can be with it at all—even if this means just our knowing it ourselves. It is like the to-and-fro of living. There must be this movement, for one movement alone would be incompatible with life, physical or otherwise.

I would like to share the following with you. These are feelings I can only be alone with.

> *My fondnesses, all,*
> *crash into one*
> *drop of dew.*
>
> *This is, of now,*
> *My being.*
> *Tomorrow?*

"A life rooted in truth"

I write this to you as my way of letting you know that
my silence and reserve and isolation are only indirectly related
to the way in which we have communicated lately.

I am presently engaged in a kind of self-consciousness and
awareness that I have not known before. It is a process of inner
searching that grows out of questions and issues that are now
confronting me. I know you think I am interested only in
finding my own private way, that I am looking for a life of
freedom and independence but this is not the basis of my
loneliness. What I am searching for is a life fully rooted in
truth and in authenticity, yet I am living with contradictions
and dishonesty that leave me feeling helpless and alone.

Just last week a problem arose that required . . . people
here [to] say what they knew. I called out to them, for
someone to speak. Forty people—some friends of long standing—and no one answered. Thus I appeared confused,
misinformed, unreal. I felt totally alone and keenly conscious
of my isolation, not belonging on this earth of normal people.

For the first time I became aware of how ridiculous my
values are, aware of the solitary nature of my actions. There
was no other way but to become numb to the lie that was there
before me, in the presence of people who did not have the guts
to speak openly, whose fear of consequences was more

powerful than their commitment to the truth. Suddenly I felt the precious nature of my solitary presence and I walked out. I began to consider every relationship in terms of moral principles. What began to surface were opposing wishes and wills glossed over and actions that challenged my dedication to honesty. If I feel lonely must I pretend social interest? If I feel placid or unalive must I feign excitement? Many everyday activities came into view. And I have developed a self-consciousness, checking to determine if what I am saying and doing is consistent with what I am feeling and who I am. I'm sure you know this is a painful process, not only in my own suffering but in the grief it brings to others. I trust this solitary struggle and believe that ultimately a more fully honest life with others will emerge. Am I searching for something that doesn't exist? Will I finally admit that an absolutely moral life is impossible? I do not know. I do not know where I am going—only that I must remain with this struggle and let it take me where it will.

I know you are aware that something extreme is happening to me and that you are suffering because my withdrawal strikes at the heart of our relationship and you are unable to reach me.

I deeply regret the pain my loneliness brings you and bear something of your suffering within myself. I feel a tenderness and love for you but my search for a truthful way to live in all my moments must take its own course before I will again feel the joy of life and the beauty of being with others.

C.M.

"My defenses had made me lonely"

I have just finished reading your book, *Loneliness*, and I feel compelled to write to you. I have read many of your other books and have found them very insightful: at first I thought because they helped me become a more sensitive nursery school teacher, but now I know it is because they helped me become stronger in responding to my self. *Loneliness* was especially meaningful because it helped me put into words and understand an experience I had with loneliness which I feel is a little different than those you described. It is the quality of openness of your own feelings that you share with your readers that prompts me to want to share my experience with you.

As I worked with little children and struggled to help them accept their feelings and to build their selves, it became apparent to me that I was not in contact with my own feelings. I went into therapy with a psychoanalyst and discovered among other things that I had lost my self early in life and had been living dead while alive . . . I was so lost from my own feelings and needs that I had spent my whole life trying to find something worthwhile about myself through praise from others. The slightest criticism would send me into despair for days. I had hidden from myself my true value and strengths because it was too painful to assume any responsibility for my self. The whole dependency-hostility depression permeated my life for years and years.

At one point in therapy I became stuck in self hatred and talked, and longed for, suicide for a long time. My depression deepened and deepened. I made myself more and more miserable, hoping desperately that my therapist would plead with me to change for his sake. No matter what I said or how I acted he silently refused to accept this responsibility. Then one day he became exasperated with me (whether or not this is a "technique" or whether I had elicited some countertransference in him I don't know or care). The result was an emotional explosion within me. I felt absolutely abandoned and alone: he, too, had not lived up to my expectations of him. The grief I felt was crushing: there was no one, no one at all who cared for me. The anguish I felt is hard to convey. My whole being was deadened, even my arms and legs were leaden, and my mind was paralyzed. . . . I was possessed by a whirling torment of loneliness, and finally, when I could express myself, there came from me an eerie, animalistic moaning. This noise was the only way I could break through the suffocating horror I felt. I could hear this voice coming from inside me but it wasn't me—it was a searing, anguished, guttural growl that seemed bigger than all of life and yet at the same time so expressive of all human sadness and loneliness. It helped to make that sound.

Later that same day I was able to realize that there was no one but me. If I didn't care for myself, then no one could. Whether or not someone cared for me could never change me. Reluctantly, oh, so reluctantly, I had to admit that I had a self. I had reached the lowest point of all, and, lo and behold, there I found my self. I didn't love that self then, I had fought against it for too long, but I begrudgingly, fearfully, wholeheartedly began to accept it, and amazingly enough, began to feel a soaring freedom. At that point I began the painful trek upward. All the anger I then directed to my therapist I could see I had directed to my self all my life. No wonder I had been lost. As I have become stronger, and less afraid, I guess, of being made alone if I act according to the needs of my self, I am able to like that self more and more. Every day I learn to trust it and rely on it more and more, and even as I describe this process to you, I am aware of joy.

My therapist and I discussed at great length the phenomenon which had taken place, but it was not until I read your book that I was able to understand that it was LONELINESS that I had been afraid of. I had to experience it to lose my dread of it and to begin to understand the deliverance it offers. My defenses had made me lonely all my life. They had put a filter between me and reality, between me and true communication and companionship with others, between me and accepting the love I inspire in others, between me and truly experiencing life and my place in it.

"Affirming our faith in our own being"

Today I read your book, *Loneliness*. It was one of those rare experiences that seem to come "just in time." Somehow I wanted you to know that I appreciated your sharing with me the feelings and insights expressed in this book—for you see it is not just a book but a kind of communication not often experienced.

The greatest value I received from sharing this communication was that when circumstances of life seem to be taking from us our right to be then we must reaffirm our faith in our own being and refuse to be pushed aimlessly along. Thank you for giving some impetus to this reaffirmation.

"I am a lone figure"

I work at night in a service station, on the graveyard shift. I clean the place. Sometimes at night I feel I am all alone in the world, standing in pitch darkness, trying to clean all that is dirty. No matter how much you clean, there is always more dirt, and more dirt, and more dark nights, more loneliness, more and more. I feel I am a lone figure becoming swallowed up by the darkness.

If I am silent, locked in a shell, if I appear retiring and a bore, if I seem withdrawn, unreachable, shattered, empty; if I seem to be tearful, sad, quiet; if I do not respond with enthusiasm; if I seem dying in my ways; if I seem secluded; if I seem bitter; if I seem simple, and at times too gentle; if I seem that way, do not reproach, do not scorn, as this is the one way left in which I can preserve some sense of self-respect, preserve some room for myself that won't be shattered, won't be destroyed; that won't give up; that dares not die; that wants to still live. If there is only silence, only in this way can I still be myself; still hang on to a piece, a thread, a slight connection with life, with sanity, before I fall to pieces, before the darkness sets in and envelopes me completely before blackness covers my world. I want to remain quiet and burst forth into the vibrant, multivaried colors of a new dawn, sprinkled with the freshness of wet rain, for in silence there is a growing that takes place; in silence there is a birth about to be born; and in the darkness there is dawn.

"A little boy part of me"

I want to say something about your book, *Loneliness.* I was the son of an army officer, and I went to West Point and spent seven years in a very numb and lonely existence as an army officer. It was during a time of intense loneliness that I first discovered and read your book, *Loneliness*, four and a half years ago. I had just split with my wife after ten years of marriage and I was very deeply into experiencing that tragic loss for the first time. Loneliness had been an emotion which I had always managed to outrun. I had discovered that if I did something important or impressive that people would make a fuss over me and I would not have to experience my own loneliness. Additionally, at age five, I became "man of the house" when my father left for World War II, leaving me in charge of my mother and telling me to take care of her and to "be good" and he would hurry home. I tried so hard to "be good," yet he didn't come home for four years. I didn't burden my mother and kept my loneliness deep within myself. On a lake in New Hampshire, when loneliness literally caught up with me after having outrun it for so long, I cried deeply; I went beneath the veneer of my tough shell and found a whole new part of the essence of me—a creativity. I wrote poems and a book and painted. And more important, I discovered a little boy part of me that had grown up early—a tenderness which

West Point didn't exactly nourish. I find that this tender part of me, rather than the tough part, was a part my friends and I both cherish. I then discovered that rather than my toughness being my strength, as I had misconstrued it in the military, it was really my tenderness that was my strength.

"Keeping faith with a high vision"

In response to your letter, long ago I saw that suffering was inevitable. It is a thing one cannot escape from unless one hides from life. Do you think for a moment that when I see what I do see of human sorrow that I should want to take the easy road? I ask nothing better than to be allowed the very high privilege of writing with my heart's blood. . . . I can only ask that I may suffer for these things which are high and brave and lovely and that I may not be weak when suffering comes. For the end success, failure, ruin or achievement I think that it matters so little. The stuff of life that matters is experience. I ask that I may be permitted to love much, to serve to the utmost limit of my capacity and to keep faith with that high vision which we call God. I shan't do it wholly. Nobody does that. I only want never to stop caring.

"To be a whole man again"

Before any more time slips by, may I write and try to express my thanks to you for [helping] me be able to be a whole man again. I was deeply touched by your book, *Loneliness*, and I thank you for what it said.

My dad is now on his bed of loneliness, dying of cancer. It's strange how all these years I've been with my dad, that only this year have I been able to tell him I love him and to embrace him; and yet I've wanted to for so many years but always felt restrained by the mores of our country. I was able to express to my dad that all our experiences together can never be taken away and that their meanings are only between us. I now weep unashamed because this is what I feel.

"When one who once listened chose not to hear"

Strange how, with the quiet peace of being alone . . . I am always aware of the pain of separation. Even stranger is that with you, the aloneness turns to loneliness and I am one with the separateness.

. . . of all those I have ever known, only you were able to hear my crying through the laughter, see my tears as I smiled. Only you ever came and touched me saying: "It is lonely, isn't it?" . . . understanding all I felt within . . . you gave me the gift of flight—the method, not the ability, and with it came the realization of how very lonely . . . how heavy deep inside one feels, when one is free . . .

My greatest loneliness comes not from others . . . it comes from *within*—a cry from the deepest part of me . . . and it cried up the loudest that one moment you ceased to listen to it. It hurts so to be apart from others, lonely because they hear me not. But what can ever come close to the pain, the brokenness inside me that was created when one who once listened . . . once heard . . . once understood, chose not to hear—and stopped listening?

"An enthusiasm for death"

How can I reassure you that what is happening to me is neither frightening, nor evil, nor sad, nor a denial of what we believe about growth and being, nor a waste of life and energy? It just had to be—it's another life experience. I feel sure that I suffer least of all, being in the midst of it all—being granted a kind of understanding and faith in, even an *enthusiasm* for death. The formula for living with the idea comes with it. It surprises me that the news is so distressing to others . . . but I am deeply touched that it matters so much to you.

At first when I suspected the possibility of cancer (when the doctor asked that I bring Dick to his office as soon as we could . . .), I thought I would not share this . . . news with those I care about—that I would stoically carry the burden as [long] as possible myself. But as time passed I decided that one shares even the misfortunes of life, and that [my] cheerful countenance . . . was false. Then, too, I can't feel that kind of separateness from others who care (and I suffer even with those who can't care). The cancer was not only mine growing out of some maladjustment in my own life, but was as much a manifestation of the suffering of humanity in our time. Being open to it (the tensions and distress of people generally) and being the kind of person in whom emotional disturbance results in physical disorder, I got the cancer, though it wasn't only mine. Not knowing what would be required of me in the endurance of pain, in making the transition to another kind of existence, or in combatting the cancer, I felt that I wanted to share the news because I needed the moral support of those who could give it. Following these feelings proved to be exactly the right thing to do. If I had died, or if instead a miracle prolonged my life until another time, the experience was so rich and basic that I never regretted sharing it. The benefits to all concerned were positive.

I wish there were time to write all of the feelings, ideas, and the reactions of others that accompanied, or rather followed, the doctor's death sentence. With those who were open, it was only necessary to acknowledge the imminence of death, shed a few tears together over the sorrow of parting and then we could enjoy our conversation. With others it was necessary to help them to accept the fact that each (not only me) lives with death constantly—that there was no guarantee that I would be the first to go—the only difference was that I *knew* with some degree of certainty the time and manner of my passing. With those who couldn't accept death, it was necessary to point out that I didn't mind it—that I had lived *more* in the years I had been here than most people would live in 90 years—I was satisfied—I had been lucky. There were many who would die without ever having lived at all—*then* death would be sad—but not for me. And I was lucky, too, to have a family to care for me. A friend of mine on the same floor had had to leave to get back to her teaching even though she had a malignant growth. She was all alone. And I also felt lucky that I had time to put my affairs in order, to say good-bye to friends, and to be free from pain because of medical advances. I would just gradually disappear. I began to become quite eager for the departure, even though I was experiencing life with a keenness and depth I had never known before. I knew that my new existence would surpass anything I had ever known.

One of the saddest experiences was when a very tight, inexpressive wife of a . . . research specialist came in. I knew she wanted to talk frankly about what was happening, but all she could find to say coherently was that she had come to talk with me about our getting a nominating committee organized to elect a new president for the Children's Matinee Series (since I would no longer be *it*). There was no way to help her and she felt miserable.

I am enjoying days of leisure and a peak creative period. Have been making mobiles and am starting some wire sculpture and am thrilled by the quality of my work. The sensitivity pays off in my work—sensitivity to what is right, what is true, what is good. At the same time I am almost in agony because I am equally sensitive to what is ugly, false, superficial, . . . disconnected, irrelevant, wasteful of human life and energy. I find most people endurable only in small doses. The problem is not how to accept death but how to accept *life!*

"In the event of my death"

One moment your hand was warm in mine and then you were gone. The door closed between us and you were taken away. Shut off in another world I felt the cold vacancy. Alone, silent and still, waiting the long loneliness.

In your hospital room, I opened your box of stationery and the words "In the event of my death" leapt out at me. Quickly I shut the box. I have been waiting now more than two hours for you to return from major surgery. The terror and dread is increasing and gripping my heart. I do not know what life will be for me if you die. I envision that now but only vague, empty images form in my mind. One thing is clear, your being in the world has brought a unique value into my life as it has for many others. I never knew it would be like this, alone, facing the painful intimacy of the dying of another person. Always before you were with me. We faced your suffering together. Who will I be in that final step, absolutely alone?

I am listening to approaching footsteps in the hall. Where are you now? What is happening in this moment? I see you there stretched out with many faces hovering over you. I see the machines and the instruments that surround you. All of it comes together in horror and I close this door.

I am waiting, trying to feel some hope. Will you come soon? Will your face tell me your ordeal is over? Hardly a night has passed these last months when I have not awakened to the depth of your suffering. In the days, I pause momentarily and stop and stare. In crowded streets I feel your hurt. And in the morning sun your pain is continuous. Yet through it all you have maintained a loving heart, a gentle spirit, and strength that has encouraged others to go on living.

When you return, let there be no more pain. Let there be only tenderness and life. As I listen for the sounds that will bring you back, this is my fervent hope—that fear and anguish and dying are finished and will never again hover over you.

C.M.

"I had to accept her illness as terminal"

While reading your book, *Loneliness*, I discovered a beautiful insight into the human soul. Through your examples and emotions I have become aware of the loneliness we experience as human beings. You have helped me realize the truth that no one can actually experience the deep emotions another person feels. Your words have forced me to search further within myself and accept the feelings I had repressed and refused to remember.

Although I had begun to think of my little girl's illness, all the truly disturbing memories continued to remain within. I had still not allowed myself to pry too deeply. While reading *Loneliness*, I was suddenly confronted with my own experiences and emotions. Spontaneously I began to think about her illness in terms of something real that had occurred in my life; I relived all the memories that had previously been buried.

As I am remembering these experiences with Teresa, I feel a tremendous need to relate how I feel. I do not want to suppress these thoughts any longer. They are so very real to me and I must express them to someone.

Since you have become a significant part in my self-awareness and have helped me to become a more real person, I wish to express my feelings to you.

Only Teresa knew the torment of her pain and somehow

endured it. No one else could feel the terror she was experiencing. I would speak to her, love her, and attempt to make her feel a little more comfortable but I could never experience her distress. Her violent convulsions and moans were constant. I can still hear her desperate cries, pleading for help. Her only relief was in her medication that would calm her for a short time and the pain would resume. Her little face that had been so beautiful and alive slowly became full of all the terror she was feeling. Her eyes revealed all the agonies. I cannot describe the heartache I felt. All my love, my heart, my soul went to her; I wanted so desperately to help her, but there was very little I could do to eliminate her despair.

The process in which this disease destroys the mind and body is heartbreaking. Her body would become completely rigid, her head would lean backwards creating a sort of backward arc. Using all my strength I would move her head forward, relieving some of the strain in her rigidness, thus making her more placid. This would be only temporary help and soon she would become rigid again. It was during these periods when her body was rigid and strained that she seemed to be in the most pain.

Often her lungs would fill with fluid and she would develop pneumonia. Each time this happened she was hospitalized. Fortunately I was allowed to remain with her day and night. Her treatments in the hospital were terrifying to her, and I don't think I could have left her to face those alone. I shall always remember the hospital staff and the doctors that were involved with Teresa, how warm and understanding they were. They too were unable to refrain from becoming emotionally distressed when observing her terrible pain. Also, I will always praise Mt. Zion Hospital and its policy to accommodate mothers if this is their wish. Teresa's days in the hospital would have been far more frightening if I was not there when she needed me. I am tremendously thankful that I was allowed to remain with her.

Words cannot adequately describe the empathy and compassion I experienced during those years. Each stage of her degeneration had been predicted, leaving me with no hope for her recovery. I had to accept her illness as being terminal.

Often she developed fantastically high fevers that could only be lowered by constant bathings in tepid water. The fevers also created a great deal of pain. . . . Each time she was hospitalized I thought it would be her last and her suffering over. I prayed and prayed to God to let her torment cease and allow her to find peace. My prayers were not answered for what seemed an eternity. Every part of me felt her pain; my heart, my body, my very soul wanted to help her, to somehow make her aware of how I knew she was suffering and that I too was feeling her pain deep within my heart.

As she lost her eyesight and became completely immobile, I could never really be certain of how much she was aware of my [physical] presence. Yet somehow I feel she was always aware of my love, my warmth, and my compassion. I hope within her heart and soul she knew that she was deeply loved by every heart that took care of her and tried to ease her pain. In reliving those years of despair, I weep for all the pain and suffering she had to endure; I weep for a beautiful angel that had experienced fantastic terror. My heart is filled with anguish as I remember the horrible ending to her life.

Her lungs had filled beyond further help; her stomach could no longer function properly and she could not be fed orally any longer. The only other alternative was intravenous feedings. My husband and I consulted with her doctors about her condition and were advised that no further feedings be given. However, the final decision was ours. Our final decision to discontinue all further feedings took all our strength.

Although we were aware it was the only human thing to do, we also knew that while we watched her take her last breaths we too would be dying within ourselves.

We drove her to the hospital for the last time. As I held Teresa in my arms I knew that this memory would remain within my heart eternally. The memory of that trip and the finality that it possessed still feel so real to me. When we arrived at the hospital I laid her gently in her bed, . . . never to hold her in my arms again. Later I tried to hold her again but she became extremely rigid in the process of lifting her. She was most comfortable and placid in bed. I knew then, she could no longer endure living [with] great pain she had known. She was ready to leave us. There was nothing more we could do for her but allow her to leave. Two days later Teresa died. Although we were near her, she died alone, unaware of another human being. She had been under heavy sedation and [was] unable to communicate with anyone. Her days of torment and agony were over.

Teresa has left us, but her memories will always remain alive and real in our hearts. She left deepest feelings of compassion and love in all the souls that loved her so dearly.

At last, all the despair and repressed emotions have been revealed as I truly feel. I feel ecstatically elated to suddenly realize that I want to think about my experiences with Teresa. I want to talk about her and write about her, but I never want to forget her memories again.

Her pleasant memories as well as her tragic memories are embedded within my being. She is a part of me and very real in my mind. I want to mold her experiences and allow them to enhance my life and my understanding of other human beings. Only then will her life have had meaning and her agonies and pain not suffered in vain.

Although I am not adequately trained in writing and my

vocabulary is limited, I have tried to relate my feelings as they have appeared to me.

By accepting and submitting to my own loneliness, new and beautiful values have been revealed. Most significant to me are your words, "We must learn to care for our own loneliness and suffering and the loneliness and suffering of others, for within pain and isolation and loneliness one can find courage and hope and what is brave and lovely and true in life."

"Each of us dies wrapped in a yellow robe"

I grieved too, for the loneliness of her living and the loneliness of her dying. I grieve at the death all about us in this hospital community—the unfructified lives wasting without the sustenance of commitment, of responsibility, of engagement, of love. I grieve that the sweet smell of spring earth goes unnoticed and that the sow bug is met with indifference. I grieve that we do not think of things in themselves and that we fill our days with influencing others, that we allow what we stand for to be more important than who we are. I grieve that we sell our birthrights for symbols of power and spurious control, and so we die without having lived. I grieve that the gift of life falls awkwardly from our trembling hands. Each of us dies wrapped in a yellow robe; and it seems we can only weep in tortured impotence before the caricature of who we might have been.

"Drawn toward the lonely"

I read your beautifully written book, *Loneliness*, and was very impressed with its truthfulness. I do believe . . . that the subject matter has been expounded many times by many writers and authors, but because of [my] lack of a formal education I never realized that anyone could possibly see me in these dimensions. I think I know the meaning of this subject as well as, if not better, than most. I need no formal education for this. I have lived, associated . . . [and] become drawn toward the lonely, and readily know those who are.

"You know I am with you"

I am writing this letter as a way of coming to terms
with the strong and powerful feelings I experienced the last
time we met. Something is still very much alive in me of the
pain of your leaving home, of your not knowing you could ever
come back. Each time I tried to speak to you I choked inside
and the words never came. I wanted somehow to let you know
that I really understood how you struggled to say farewell to a
world you have known from your beginnings, a world of
tenderness and caring, how you struggled to face the feeling
that that world may never exist again for you. One day your
life was intact. Your family was fully there for you. The next
moment this human support was sharply and suddenly gone. I
felt the loss, too, and wondered what would happen to your
basic innocence and trust, to what you've always been able to
count on. I wanted to reach you, to let you know that I was
there in that shattering awareness of roots left behind, of
facing a confusing world alone. I wanted to offer you
something that you could take with you into that darkness and
uncertainty. But all I could do was to be there with you in the
cold, rainy night, on a strange street with cars and people
rushing around us and all the loud noises. There were no
words in me to offer you courage and strength. I know that
you know I am with you in whatever you do to find a life that

will bring you joy and fulfillment. And though I know you must create that world on your own it is hard to live with this truth, with all the barriers and obstacles that others will put before you.

I wanted to tell you then and I want to tell you now that you have always been here in my heart and you always will be, that what we have lived and known will be there waiting for you to come home to, a permanent place in you, in me, in others who have held you and helped you grow in your own way.

You did not want to make that final moment final. You took my hand strongly in yours. I felt the love flowing between us as you held onto that last instant and then you were gone.

None of this is really saying what's in my heart tonight—YOU—your music, your joking ways, how you enter a room and stand, your quickness, your putting everything you've got into what matters to you, what you've grown yourself through steady persistence, what we've shared together all these years. It's all here in me now. It has enriched my life, making sense of the absurdity, bringing light into the darkness, contributing to my life as a human being.

This love goes with you into that unknown world you are now entering. It will be there as a steady presence when you face the problems and issues of living and it will shine like a beacon to light your way back home.

C.M.

"I fought the terror of life"

I have bought your book *Loneliness* today. Now at 3:00 in the morning after reading it I feel that I must write to you. You, a person whom I have never seen, have become a friend.

I must tell you that I know of the meaning of loneliness, from the terrors of a suicidal manic-depressive to a half-alive person who is now starting to live with joy and strength.

Now nineteen, I have felt the total aloneness that comes from mental illness, the wish of death when at sixteen I did not even know of life. Then with the love of my parents, their support . . . , and . . . people like you, I tried to turn towards life after seeing death. I know the loneliness of falling and trying once again, the beauty of being alone and seeing the sun rise after I have fought the terror of life.

Thank you for your book. Tonight you were here with me as I again tried to face life.

"Afraid to be lonely"

I read those parts from *Loneliness* which I felt a need to read during Christmas vacation. I was deeply affected by the experiences I was able to share. I picked the book up again and read and was surprised at the wonderment of being able to experience as though never before these same journeys through loneliness.

I felt that my very feelings were caught up and understood by the author—that a friendly someone could write what I had felt, but hadn't been able to express in words.

I gained something from this reading, partly that I don't have to feel that being lonely is wasteful—that I don't have to be busy every minute, to be a complete person. Before I was afraid to be lonely, afraid I was just wasting precious time and afraid that I wasn't adequate . . . within myself.

For someone who usually rambles endlessly on when affected by something, I can't really think of anything else to say; perhaps later, right now I'm still experiencing it.

"The shock of divorce"

I suppose in all I have written, in what I have felt these last few weeks, even in apartment hunting, is the slowly emerging, yet inevitable process of the shock of eventual divorce which really dwindles a good deal of hope; I'm not sure when it will come, yet I know it will. There doesn't seem to be any panic or fear anymore, just a very dull sense and emotional preparation which has completed itself. This is a hard process to go through for anybody. You try to grasp onto all sorts of threads. Even though you say to yourself, I'm doing everything now as a single person, emotionally you know underneath. In every respect, you're saying to yourself, will this please her, . . . and will this help the children; and then you realize they are no longer with you, . . . It's not the loneliness, not the shock, not the fear, not the sense of failure, but the sense of a dying, of a relationship dying, and no one can stop it, not really—not yourself, your work, your money, your efforts, your hopes, your dreams; not your realities, not your friends, not anybody. And then you know that there will be more grief to come, more hard realities to face, probably more hurt; and you pray, you pray that in the breakdown of your home, your family, your relationship with your wife, that in some way your children may find enough strength to endure and grow—[be]cause that's where the real guilt and sense of failure lies. . . . You know you can never repair what has been broken; it's to the children, not anybody else that you have a responsibility. It's them you need to feel for, not mama or daddy, not really; it's to them that the dawn must speak and comfort and help grow; it's to them that hopefully out of the mess, their goodness might survive.

"Alive enough to die"

I have just finished reading your book *Loneliness*, and even while I was reading it I wanted to write [to] you. I think that the high value which you place on the experience of loneliness is just, for I feel that anything which I know or understand comes from my own experiences of loneliness or from my empathy for others undergoing such experiences.

Looking back on my own childhood I think it must have been very lonely—at least all the requirements were there— and yet I was never aware of it as such; I couldn't have possibly called it by that name. When I was about seven years old I spent several months in the hospital with no real understanding of the situation. I was given shots every four hours; I sometimes had several blood transfusions per day. I later learned that it was thought I might not live.

This isn't what I want to talk about though, and I don't know if it's relevant. Several years ago I spent two summers trying to be alone. I lived alone; the first summer on a farm in Vermont, the second summer in Cambridge, Massachusetts. It was unsuccessful, though I did learn some things. I didn't succeed in being alone partly because I didn't extricate myself from people enough, partly because I wasn't so sure I wanted to be after all, and partly because there was some pressure from my parents for me to give up this scheme. The result was a compromise. I really stayed more or less as I was. I recognized a need for being close to myself, of confronting myself, of learning who I was, but situations were not propitious; there was always an artificiality about what I was doing.

Two things changed that: one was my decision to undergo psychoanalysis, and the other was an intimate relationship with a girl. Both of these were for me acute and unavoidable confrontations of myself with myself. Both were quite painful, particularly the relationship with the girl, for I felt that she never really accepted me as I was (perhaps this was mutual), and yet I could not break off either. And at the same time I never experienced such violence of emotion—love or hate— except perhaps when I was very young, up to the age of twelve. Feelings which I never suspected of having in me welled up to overwhelm me, often feelings of lust or hate.

It is impossible for me to really feel again those feelings as I sit here at the typewriter. I know they happened, some as recently as two or three months ago, and yet to recall them is exceedingly difficult. Partly because they are part of a whole complex which I would probably prefer submerged out of the picture. At the same time I know that when I read poetry now I respond with more feeling and understanding than before all this happened.

Now isn't that strange! I was just going to write that I never really sought challenge, that it always seemed to come by accident. I can't tell for sure if that's true or not, but I had completely forgotten an experience that happened to me this summer. I went down on foot into the bottom of the Grand Canyon. It's hard for me to really believe that I could have been totally unaware of what I was getting in for, and yet I acted that way. I took with me a camera, a few biscuits, and a small canteen of water; I ended up walking, with occasional rest periods, for 14 or 15 hours, with next to no food or water. Why did I do it? I have no understanding of it, and yet in writing you just now connections are forming in my mind. It was senseless, stupid, if you will, and yet had I been guided by sense I would have avoided this experience.

I have rarely wanted (or perhaps I have had the want beaten out of me) to communicate my inmost thoughts to others, because I know that they won't understand. I have very rarely withheld my sympathy from anyone, but I just now wonder if that isn't some kind of compensation for the fact that I do withhold other things.

. . . For a while now, I don't know how long exactly, I have felt prepared to die. By that I don't mean at all that I want to (though I have felt that too), but rather that I was alive enough to die. I went through a long period when I was very anxious about death. But this past week I looked at the stars, and somehow realized that I could accept my death as mine. I can almost feel with Camus' Stranger that there is a kind of pleasure in knowing that my death is waiting for me somewhere.

"To be in touch with myself"

Of course I feel as if I know you. That you could be in a crowd and I would just know and yell HELLO! HOW ARE YOU TODAY? and really be concerned with your answer.

I read *Loneliness*. Then I bought copy after copy for friends. Sometimes sharing my own copies with people that are very special to me. My books are marked with RIGHT! I UNDERSTAND! and YES! All that you have shared (at times it must have been very painful) has been to me exciting, alive, and authentic. However, my favorite line is, "But while a person is struggling in lonely silence to find his way back to life again, to give birth to a new path that comes from within to restore his spirit and passion for life, he needs strong, unqualified, affirming voices. . . ."

I would like to tell you that you have given me those voices. When it seemed, and indeed was true, that my life was dissolving around me you were there. I was choosing myself over my reflection of self and you were there. When I decided that, whatever the price, I had to be in touch with myself, had to follow my own instincts, you were there. My strong, unqualified, affirming voice.

I thank you. And since our spirits have met I would like to call you friend, knowing, of course, that since you do not know me that you cannot feel the same. But how can I share so much with someone and still think of him as only a name?

"To feel all the way
into a moment"

After receiving a telephone call that one of my graduate students was involved in an auto-train collision and was in the hospital in a coma, I went off alone and sat silently for several hours. Though I knew there was no way of speaking directly to Doris, the following letter emerged as my way of responding to the tragedy:

I feel strange writing this to you knowing you are in the hospital, in a coma, unable to read or hear, unable to respond. I feel strongly the desire to communicate with you and believe somehow even now we are in touch, in a spiritual sense.

Glenn's call was an absolute shock. I cannot imagine it. I feel inside a sickness—so many times this year I have wanted to pause to say I have felt your honesty, your gentle nature, your inner beauty. Perhaps you knew even though we have met only briefly lately.

I do not want to let myself feel all the way into this present moment; it is filled with too much horror, and the pain is overwhelming. I cannot fully believe it; I cannot understand it, but intensely I feel the hope of your recovery, your return to health.

I close my eyes and for a moment I am with you there, in the struggle. The snow falls gently outside, and the dark black branches of the trees move slightly in the wind. I feel your smile and your love. I know the goodness of your person. Oh, Doris, I am sorry that you must suffer so.

I think of you. I'll wait for you. I dream of your return.

My heart is with you; the strength of my spirit and my love too.

C.M.

"When I have touched another life"

I have been so deeply moved by my reading of *Loneliness* that I just had to write now, however incoherent the result may be.

I am a sixth grade teacher in the ghetto of Venice (Los Angeles), where, this past year, I have had an "open classroom." I feel that the changes in the children justify my courage, pain and loneliness, but it is still *very* difficult. As I become more myself, I find I need less and less structure in the classroom—and that means more problems with the administrator and the system. My willingness and then eagerness to change my teaching style have evolved over the last two years, within a context of enormous changes in my personal and inner lives (divorce after 15 years of marriage, a subsequent relationship which started me on *my* investigation of loneliness) and a life-long interest in civil liberties and the philosophy of freedom.

I always like to know when I have touched another's life—I thought you would like to know how deeply you have touched mine.

"Loneliness—an antidote to surface living"

I have just finished reading your most thoughtful and poetically written book, *Loneliness*. I had heard about it in Israel where I have been living for some years, although [I was] born and educated in Baltimore, Buffalo, and at Columbia University in New York City. So when I returned recently to the U.S.A., I immediately ordered your book. It has reestablished for me confidence in some Americans' ability to *feel*, for I have been astounded with finding many of my relatives, friends, and acquaintances indulging in surface living.

Also, your wise and philosophical ideas which you so clearly expound have given me a better understanding of many Israelis, those who have come to Israel as a place of refuge after suffering hellish tortures in other lands. Maybe it is as you say: "Loneliness has a quality of immediacy and depth, it is a significant experience—one of the few in modern life—in which man communes with himself. And in such communion man comes to grips with his own being. He discovers life, who he is, what he really wants, the meaning of his existence, the true nature of his relations with others. He sees and realizes for the first time truths which have been obscured for a long time.

His distortions suddenly become naked and transparent. He perceives himself and others with a clearer, more valid vision and understanding."

"The darkness in me touches you"

In facing the dying of an intimate friend, the following letter, written to myself, came after waking in the middle of the night and walking until dawn.

I will not participate in the gaiety around me when in my heart I know you are alone.

I do not know the meaning of joy when I see the sadness in your eyes.

I speak but the words embrace a darkness that no bright sun can invade.

My footsteps are weighted with not knowing.

You move with a willingness and enter swiftly the dark clouds, the rainy nights and the setting suns.

You merge easily with distant stars.

I refuse to submit. I continue to live in conflict, stumbling, not knowing the way.

I wonder if the darkness in me touches you and increases your suffering. For me, there is no substitute—only the pain fully expresses my love.

I know that when the time comes I will go with you into the unknown, not quietly but strongly protesting the injustice with every fiber of my being.

C.M.

"The no-choice reality
of going alone"

I started *Loneliness* late one night when I was tired of studying and deep in the throes of a loneliness trip of my own—different than I had ever experienced—terrifying yet somehow good in its simple realness. As I read the beginning, my only reaction was shock because one of our children, the oldest, eight years old, has a congenital heart defect which is operable today only at high risks; and we live with the knowledge that he could get worse at any time. He has just begun to get to the stage of trying in some way to deal with its beginning to restrict him a little and with the questions of why it happened to him—the unanswerables—and I [am] to the stage of having honestly told him as much as I can and given as much love and support as I can. . . . No matter how open we are and how he knows that we are honest with him and love him and wish it weren't so . . . he . . . must in some way find a way to accept it, live with it, incorporate it somehow. . . . He must do it by himself in his own time, in his own way; . . . I can hold his hand, feel some of it with him but can never do it *for* him or feel what he feels— . . . In this he is really alone and . . . no matter how much honesty and love flows between us, the gap, the loneliness exists—where he has to come to terms with it and I [to terms] with being powerless to cut through his struggle and ultimate aloneness. Your willingness to communicate your experience somehow clarified what I was struggling with in the days before his check-up, and somehow when the questions came I was able to answer better, more comfortably than ever before and to accept the no-choice reality of the way he has to go alone. Your book was not a book to read—it was an experience I lived and felt, and I can only say "thank you" for sharing the terror and beauty and reality of your experiences and feelings of loneliness.

"Reaching my truth is a high priority"

This letter has been long in finding expression and I hope it reaches you. You've enriched my life in many ways and I want to say that to you.

Never having been a child myself and having chosen (part voluntary and part "fate") to be a loner in life, your words (you through them) help me struggle from the non-me-me to the season of my life when reaching my truth is a high priority.

Most fruitful is the sharing of yourself and finding time, waiting, respecting self and others so essential. The distinguishing between truth enduring and temporal honesty is where I'm at. Groups can be a real crucifixion!

Through your words I can struggle with continued effort and appreciate where I am. I find it *fatal* to compare myself with others but very humbling and a grateful and positive experience comparing me *only* to me. My thanks. May your seasons of loneliness be fruitful!

"Creating a stream of sensitivity"

Tonight I have been reading your book *Loneliness* and although I have only read to page 54 I felt an intense desire to write you this letter. I must tell you that your book has and will help me a great deal now and in later life.

Throughout my life I have associated with all classes of people. I have few prejudices and my greatest wealth lies in the fact that I have dear, true, faithful friends in all classes. Some of the wealthiest down to some of the poorest are my friends. I am proud to have these friends and proud of the fact that I can talk to them and speak out my heart to them, thus aiding them in some way.

However, until now I could never help myself. I wanted to feel free but I never have. Every door I ever entered led to frustration sooner or later. I always got the feeling that I did not "belong." When I made new friends and found new and interesting things to do I was happy for a while but soon I would become frustrated. I cannot control myself when it comes to spending money. I seem to always be in debt. I always seem tied down. I have always felt as though I were searching for a star that never existed. I have always been lonely! Now I want to tell you that I think your book is going to help me a great deal. It has given me confidence in myself and confidence that I can help others.

When I was a junior in high school my teacher asked the class to stand and tell what they would wish for if they had only one wish. I stood before my class and said that I wished I could be the most loved man in the world. Everyone laughed at me, but I did not care. I was sincere and their laughter did not make me ashamed. I still would like to be loved by all the people around me. I often appear to be playing two ends against the middle, because of this. I consider every human being a sacred thing. Many do not. That is my greatest complaint against the world in general. What can I do to create a stream of sensitivity in the hearts of those around me so that they might consider others?

I have a friend at school who is also lonely. We write poems and let each other read them and we are very content together.

I want to apologize for my informal writing, bluntness, and for the use of your time; however, I felt a strange urge to speak to you through a letter and so I decided to write. I hope you don't mind, and I hope you will take time to reply.

Your book has and will mean much to me and I only hope others will find themselves by exploring *Loneliness*.

"A breath of life made me whole again"

Recently your book *Loneliness* came into my hands. To read, to feel the depth of your book, was one of the really rewarding experiences of my life. In this world of superficial gestures, of sham encounters that slowly dehumanize us, your book came as a breath of life making me whole again. When I complained that other people were being insincere or manipulating me, I was always told I was "suspicious" or "maladjusted." Your book has taught me to seek out now meaningful, honest, sham-free, human encounters; it has given me confidence in my own judgments again. I no longer try to "adjust" or please the crowd. Slowly I am seeking out new friends, and losing old false friends.

The compassion you show, the genius of heart you brought to the people who turned to you for help, has changed my whole thinking about things of ultimate value in human relationships.

"People are hungry to be their own authorities"

Not long ago I talked to a group of people with considerable feeling in my presentation, pointing their attention to the need to be individual and independent centers for living, each man in his own. I had been able to suggest that this was an avenue also to deepest companionship and significant social value. After my lecture, I noticed that the group disbanded quickly and individuals went off by themselves, not even coming up to me as they usually do. My first impulse was to feel that my lecture had fallen flat. Later I learned that the opposite was the case, with several of the group at least. People are hungry to be their own authorities in basic life matters, and, spurred by my own expression in these matters, they wanted it all the more, meaning they had to leave me to my own, too.

I need not tell you that I think you are doing just the right thing in forming your experience as you are doing. The vacuum of "being," if not filled with the substance of life-realized in depth (as you are doing), will gain so much power that our people will collapse inwardly in the clutter of their own psychic debris.

"From a winter of loneliness"

I am grateful to you for creating new meaning for words which for me have long lain still, insipid, vapid, yet restless in their dormancy, anxious to take on new truth. From a winter of loneliness and solitude, friendlessness and suffering, a spring has arrived which promises the beginning of real meaning for me. I begin my search, and though I have not articulated my feelings nearly as precisely as you do in *Loneliness* I know I am with you in many of your experiences.

It is ironic that only after the completion of my graduate work do I begin to know and accept the meaning and price of growth and learning.

Thank you for sharing your loneliness and your love.

"It's like I don't belong"

It's like I don't belong, no matter where I go; somehow, as always, I am left in the cold, alone, by myself. And no matter how much I try to be myself and have friends, and be alive; each time, my friends depart, go their own way, achieve their goal, and I'm left alone. It's always been that way, ever since I can remember. As a child, I'd play alone in the backyard, planting flowers, or looking for bugs, or making patterns and designs with pieces of rock, or nails, or dirt, or paint left over from painting the rooms upstairs in the house.

I remember that if I remained alone, and played by myself, built something, or grew something, or painted—I loved to paint and crayon pictures—I'd be all right; I'd feel strong and better; night, silence, these didn't bother me at all. I never even felt I belonged in my own family, even though I turned to them so very much; even now, after my mother died, and my wife left me, I turned to my family and again the same things happened. I felt I didn't belong either to my family or in social situations; it's very tiring and I know I need to just remain by myself, that's all and try to do something, like I did as a child, and just be alone, that's all. Because in the end, that's the way it will turn out anyway, alone; yet if I can create something in the aloneness, then I'll be all right, and I won't really be alone and won't really suffer, for in being alone, you can grow.

"My feelings were step children"

It has been so short a time that I have been able to share with another the coldness, blackness, and emptiness of the void experienced as loneliness and alienation. And, deeply as I love relationship and encounter, I also need solitude to grow in another way, to regenerate and reintegrate. How many times the change within me ("insight," "solution," or simply new perspective) has come in the solitude *after* the encounter which made it possible. This has been enough different from those around me to make me feel alien at times.

My feelings were step children so long, and my heart mute. At a point in therapy I had come through a siege of depression and self-doubt during which I had looked at my dark side and shared fears and despair with another for the first time in my life. I could face life again with some joy, some hope. I felt so much but could find no words for these feelings. I stammered out something about hoping I had not been too much bother, and he communicated his love as well as his acceptance of me—ALL of me. This man who had seen my weaknesses and my negative feelings—he could care? I felt the most intense pain of my life then and sat for minutes with closed eyes, reeling under it. It hurt like pent-up life rushing into a chilled and starved soul. It was such a *good* hurting. I can't say for sure, but it was as though only when I was no longer alone and alien I could stand the pain of loneliness and the hunger of my heart for understanding, for relationship that did not *exclude* part of me. Perhaps just being so open to feeling and to immediate experiencing was painful. Only later when the experience had lost a little of its overwhelming intensity did the words of a poem pour out and I could weep with joy.

Rereading this, I hesitate—yet I believe you might understand. You are the first person who has shared with me the response to attack of pain and found that it, too, can lead to growth and resolution into relationship. For me to strike back does not ease my pain but often adds more. This is hard enough to understand for many others, but when I say that experiencing understanding, another's caring—this too can be painful—I experience such disbelief that I fall silent.

To one who has enriched my life and gladdened my heart. . . .

"I use my 'thinking dreams'"

I read *Loneliness* while I was on a vacation cruise with my family. We went on the s. s. Rotterdam. We sailed to the West Indies from New York and then back to New York. I think the environment for the reading of *Loneliness* was particularly appropriate, for I was quite lonely on the ship. Oh, there were lots of teens on board and I truly (at first) wanted to be included in their group, but after I went to a few of the teen parties, I decided that I really wasn't one of them (they knew that also, and didn't accept me, either).

I read *Loneliness* in the afternoons on deck, in the sun. There were lots of people around, swimming, talking, sleeping, etc. While I read this, I was apart from my family—I made sure of that. It's not that I don't love them, but sometimes family companionship and activities can get a little nerve-racking, and I had to get away from that and their constant harping (especially my father's "Smile!" "Don't you feel good?" "Show some life!" "What a personality!"). While I sat in the deck chair, in the sun, with *Loneliness* in my hand, I felt isolated and alone, yet content.

As I try to recall what things I liked and disliked about the book, my mind and thoughts become kind of muddled and foggy. I know that I agreed with much of what you said, and many times I said to myself "Ah, yes, that's right. . . . I often

feel that way. . . . I remember something like that." A few
examples that I recall concerned the terror of a hospital and
child fantasy. When I was in the hospital last year for four
weeks after the accident, I felt that aloneness and emptiness. I
was not terrified—I understood why things were done; but I
still felt the pain, and no one was able to share that with me. It
was an individual experience, I understood, yet I felt alone.
The other example hits close to home also—"child" fantasy.
Child is quoted because I still live in a world of fantasy.
Anytime during the day or night when I'm not actively
thinking or doing something specific, I use my "thinking
dreams"—I have a number of them; I am always a central
figure, and they usually concern someone or something I
admire and like. I really don't remember how or when they
started, but I do know they had something to do with the lack
of "participant" love I have felt all my life. By this I mean that
I know my parents love me and would do anything they could
for me, but 1) my mother has worked much of my life, and 2)
my father just doesn't understand why I do not bubble, talk,
and show emotions constantly (I really don't know that answer
either).

When I finished reading the number of pages I had time for
each day, I would usually walk around the deck, go up to the
bridge and just look at the water (or shore, if we were in port).
And, often these phrases from a song we have sung in choir
went through my mind: To dance, exult . . . Oh to realize
space—

> *the sun and moon . . .*
> *Oh to be rulers of life . . .*
> *Oh to be rulers of destiny,*
> *of life and destiny . . .*
> *We sing prophetic joys,*
> *of lofty ideals . . .*
> *Listen to the jubilant song!*

I finished the last chapter on Sunday, January 4. We were returning, and the weather was quite chilly and gloomy. The value of *Loneliness* was truly a masterpiece. I couldn't begin to give my reactions to it here—every word, every syllable was so true, so wonderful. I left the deck chair, spellbound. I went up to the ninth deck. The wind was whipping around, and the water was quite choppy. I went to the bow end of the deck; there it was enclosed by some windows. I stood. I looked. I thought about the mysterious yet marvelous sea . . . about life . . . about man and humanity . . . about me . . . about God. I was alone and lonely, but happy and warm inside.

At our table in the dining room we had the same two waiters the whole trip. Gerard was kind of special though. He always smiled at me and I smiled back—something was there, it still is. That Sunday at lunch, after I had finished my communion, he smiled again, and all of a sudden I felt different . . . I thought of this song because it says what happened better than I can:

> *Something in your smile speaks to me*
> *Something in your smile says be unafraid*
> *It shows me the way*
> *And helps me say the things I could never say. . . .*

Yes let there be loneliness, "for where there is loneliness, there also is love, and where there is suffering, there also is joy."

"The end of a beautiful melody, and of all music"

I awoke this morning to a soft and gentle rain, remembering a night not long ago when we paced back and forth while you struggled to come to terms with your dying.

I am writing to tell you how much you have given me in your presence, in your love, in your unqualified acceptance of me. When I came, you always recognized me in a distinctive way. Above all else, I felt I mattered to you. You never let anything—time, or place or person—interfere with that. So I have counted on you like the ground I walk on and the air I breathe. You were always there for me in the way the earth and the sky are always there. It simply never occurred to me that the day would come when I would no longer have your eternal faith, that for awhile I would lose the earth, the water and the air, that I would have to watch my own footsteps and accept as real the end of a beautiful melody, and of all music.

What grieves me now in this time of painful loneliness is that I never before put my feelings, my sacred valuing of you, into words! In all the other times it was always you who spoke, of how much I offered you, and all the while you were fully there for me. So I want to say clearly and strongly for now and for all the days beyond that you have given me the special gift of life itself, and I know it with my eyes and ears and with all my senses. I will always cherish the unique presence that is you.

C.M.

4
The Unknown in
Loneliness and Self–Renewal

I am writing now as a way of describing my recent experiences with loneliness and isolation, my own personal struggle and anguish, my confrontation with the unknown in loneliness and self-renewal. I want to put into words that period of two weeks in which I chose to cut myself off from others—my family and friends and all those persons with whom I had shared a life. I want to speak of the pain and the horror as well as my eventual breakthrough to new energy and life, to convey in depth something of the feelings and ideas involved and the shocking awareness and discovery of what it means to trust the unknown in guiding the way. I want to recreate those currents of feeling and thought to awaken my own awareness and being and to know that I am alive in this moment and that loneliness has helped to sustain that life.

My message is not simply in words but in the pauses between and in the sweep of feeling and mystery through which the words have been created, of which the words are only a fragment. If I were interested merely in providing knowledge that grew out of my study of loneliness, I would summarize in brief terms. But there is a crucial difference between a living process and knowledge about life. What I am sharing is the reality itself in the form that I believe is most fitting, in the hope that it will create within me a realization of my own sense of mystery, my own response to the unknown, and the opening of my inner life to the truth of this journey and all the journeys to follow.

I am remembering vividly as I write that intimate life in a strange land with people who had come to be central in my world. As the days unfolded, we shared the joys of mountain peaks, the thrill of immense, continuing surf pounding against the seashore, and glorious, colorful flowers that surrounded us everywhere. On one miraculous late afternoon we followed boiling lava down a path to the ocean, where bubble, spray, and steam rose above us and created the most exciting fireworks we had ever seen. As the sun was disappearing into the sea, we retraced our steps, while composing songs of love in communal joy. On that night especially, I was deeply moved with the wonder of life and the feeling of living within natural elemental things. At the same time a sadness overcame me, an awareness of how often people today are cut off from or indifferent to water and earth and trees.

Reading Henry Beston's *The Outermost House*, published in 1928, it was a shock to realize that this same disillusionment, hunger and awareness was felt just as strongly 46 years ago.

> The world today is sick to its thin blood for lack of elemental things, for fire before the hands, for water welling from the earth, for air, for the dear earth itself underfoot. In my world of beach and dune these elemental presences lived and had their being, and under their arch there moved an incomparable pageant of nature and the years. The flux and reflux of ocean, the incomings of waves, the gathering of birds, the pilgrimages of the sea, winter and storm, the splendour of autumn and the holiness of spring.

In those hours and days of unrest in that faraway land, it was not lack of elemental things that sickened me. With the striking beauty, with all the amazing adventures, the awesome discoveries in nature and the freedom from time pressures and schedules, something was missing. We were sharing our deepest thoughts and feelings, facing issues and conflicts that emerged in our living together, and relating with an openness, freedom and trust that encouraged each of us to pursue individual preferences in a group setting. Yet somehow thrown together as we were, there was a sense of loss.

Within hours of our gathering, the high peak of anticipation of the journey struck me. Our senses were immediately alive with strange new beauties, with smells and visions, and auditory vibrations that were everywhere. Goose bumps and prickles were brought on by broken roads, dangerous curves and frightening, precarious heights. In each day, one intense emotion after another touched our lives and brought us together, laughing, open-mouthed, struck with awe and won-der, in yelping joy, in running excitement, in music and movement, in sun and rain, in the glory of ballet in crystal-clear water. At the same time, one intense emotion after another splintered us, sent us off alone in fear, anger, silence, hurt, in search of a way to live when natural sources of communication were blocked or broken. I had believed that the presence of love would enable each of us to transcend self-interests that interfered with communal activity, that we would reach out and affirm the venture of another even though it was not our trip. I had believed that love would prevail and that connections would continue to form in spite of everything. But love did not hold us together. Love was present, but something essential was not. Gradually my spirit began to dim and, though there were outward signs of life, for a while there was nothing growing within.

When I returned from the trip, I felt an overwhelming reaction to having lived in an intense, intimate, and continu-ing life with others. I experienced a strong desire to be alone, and I deliberately cut myself off from others. I sought within, not for an answer, but for a way to live. For hours I sat silently, but nothing came. Each day I waited for the sun to rise, but only the darkness persisted.

A passage from Georges Dumas' book *The Sadness and The Joy* describes, in a vivid and powerful way, one component of my experience:

> The world now looks remote, strange. . . . Its color is gone, its breath is cold. . . . I see everything through a cloud. . . . I see, I touch but the things do not come near me, a thick veil alters the hue and look of everything. Persons move like shadows, and sounds seem to come from a distant world—There is no longer any past for me; people appear so strange; it is as if I could not see any reality, as if I were in a theatre; as if people were actors, and everything were scenery; I can no longer find myself; I walk, but why? Everything floats before my eyes, but leaves no impression.

Each day I experienced a continuing feeling of detachment and a desire to be alone, immune to life. I wanted only internal dialogue, and I believed that through an internal sign I would discover the next step. Since there were no voices within to speak to me, and no resources to begin a new journey, I spoke to the walls of my office and communed with my ceiling and the floor of my room. I waited for something to happen, for some sure way to nurture myself, to live from within. Music, art, poetry, hot baths, savory foods, wind, rain—nothing affected me. In the past, within days after a solitary retreat, I would find solace and strength in my loneliness. I had always found a way, at least a beginning that would lead to action and to life with others. But now, after many days, I was still on a lonely journey in silence, waiting for a spark from within. Because I felt empty and eroded inside, I avoided all significant communication. More than anything else the interpersonal aspects of living exhausted me and moved me to withdraw from real meetings with others. I also knew for certain that I did not want to struggle anymore.

I was tired of struggling and wanted only to know a quiet silence. What a shock this was to my own awareness of who I am. I had always considered struggle essential in growth, and in many crises and conflicts it had provided the turning point in my life. I was now turning away from it; not wanting to be burdened and overwhelmed by heavy feelings and thoughts or by complicated searching and painful unraveling of what was wrong with me, people, and life. I wanted only to be alone in simple and ordinary ways. For almost two weeks I lived in solitude and engaged only in simple routines.

Gradually, with each day, I was to be able to listen a little more to what others were saying. Slowly I began to be interested in and comfortable with other people's problems. I could be with others while they struggled to make decisions, but I was not open to questions or personal comments and responses directed to me. I offered nothing of myself and commented only on what I was hearing and understanding from others.

During this period, I found work a truly rewarding activity. In work, I felt at home with myself. It did not matter whether the work took the form of writing—reports, references, and letters—or reading. Or, if it involved physical activities, I would become totally absorbed in what I was doing, lose myself, and experience a full sense of relief. Active mental and physical involvement in solitary projects was my salvation. I believed that if I surrendered myself to powers within and sources of light in the universe, that in some mysterious way, a miracle would happen. I felt certain that a beginning was there in me. It must be. When that light revealed itself, I would be ready, too. So, I did not force or push or beseech. I simply waited with firm faith that I was meant to be whole again and that I would live once more in a full and complete way. It became clear that people I loved and those who loved me could not reach me. Life had to come from another source, and I believed the new direction would emerge in my solitude.

At this time I began reading D. H. Lawrence's *Women in Love*, and a passage of it leaped out at me. It closely fitted my own struggle to understand and come to terms with an elusive truth.

> But we want to delude ourselves that love is the root. It isn't. It is only the branches. The root is beyond love, a naked kind of isolation, an isolated me, that does *not* meet and mingle, and never can. . . . It is true what I say; there is a beyond, in you, in me, which is further than love, beyond the scope, as stars are beyond the scope of vision, some of them.

And so it was with me. What I was facing was beyond the reach of love. I knew for certain that love was not the root from which I would begin to grow again. The way back was within me. Within the darkness inside me there must be a light that would shine forth in my solitude. What it required was a naked kind of loneliness. I felt certain my life would not move forward through the caring or help of others. I was completely at home with myself in my detachment from significant communication and relationships. The fires within had died, the joys of living had diminished, yet in solitude I was convinced that something vital would emerge and awaken me.

Two things stood out—physical exertion and loneliness. These were all that mattered. I realized then that at many crucial times it is not therapy or love and understanding that move a person forward but rather what happens between meetings when the person is utterly alone. It is in this state of naked isolation and loneliness that the potential for growth and change exist, that the desire to live and to be joyous again are reborn. I saw how much we have emphasized the value of relationship and communication with others as essential in learning and in living, and how little we have encouraged and aided the individual to know the significance of solitude, how little we have recognized the significance of communion with one's self in all real living and personal growth. I came to believe that what we do not see is often what matters; invisible sources of life contain the seeds for new growth, and a profound experience of inner silence is required to start the new life. Only I could discover this new life on my own. What matters is not what others do for us but what we do for ourselves in the internal sense when we are alone with the powers of life that surround us—the stars, clouds, water, earth, and air, and senses, feelings, and awarenesses that emerge from the unknown.

In those days of isolation, I realized that out of conflict, tension, and despair a new truth arises that enables a person to return to life with others. In a time of personal crisis, it is important that the individual not seek an answer from outside. Neither friendship nor therapy can provide the awareness, direction, or shift that is required when a pattern of living is ending, when life has lost its vitality and meaning, when the person is no longer responding in depth, in a full way. In such times it is essential that the person look within, detached and isolated, that he or she be open to the unknown sources of energy in life and in the universe. The alternating rhythms of work and solitude were my salvation.

Each day I honored the simple, ordinary routines that helped me to move with real energy. Nothing mattered, yet everything did as I waited to be reborn. In the meantime, I kept faith with internal rhythms, with the integrity of my own self.

The new life came in a resounding way, not while I was alone but in a heavy stream of involvement with others. For two days I had been listening to people who were planning to work together in programs for exceptional children. Again and again, the openings were quickly closed by indifference and irrelevancy. Repeatedly, beginnings were abruptly terminated before the first real breaths were taken. Some people slept while others vainly expressed their fears and doubts. At first I was too much engrossed in my own internal struggle to intervene, but gradually the fragments and splinters and hurts began to disturb me. I experienced internally the broken moments, shattered dialogues, and cruelty of neutral faces. Here were people committed to the rescuing of "dropouts" and "rejects" from the public school, blatantly ignoring the crucial feelings being expressed.

In this room in the many passing hours and in that moment were people who hungered for a vital, active, listening human presence. But what they got were intellectual arguments and words with little or no feeling. What they got were dead faces and lifeless bodies. Within me was growing an indignation against these denials of elemental human values until at last my own existence, my own isolation, my own desire for a solitary state crumbled away and vanished. For the first time in two weeks, I was experiencing intense and vital feelings from within, a full response to others. My anger mounted at the surface way in which fundamental matters were handled, at the ignoring of potential for intensity and depth, and at people committed to serving abused and rejected children failing to reach out, recognize, and affirm each other.

It took me back to another time and place when I was meeting with a group of Catholic novitiates. Their main concern was to fulfill the requirements for becoming priests. There too, what I observed was a coldness and indifference to personal struggles and feelings, an avoidance of intensity and depth in interactions, an intellectualizing and professionalizing of religious values and concepts. Mystery, spirit, feeling, the human sense, the unspoken and ineffable, the sense of awe and wonder, aesthetic appreciation—all were missing. What else is the religious but a willingness to submit to the unknown, to learn from the unseen and intangible what we must fulfill? Where else do powers of life, actions to living in the deepest and fullest sense, come but from felt presences that awaken us to a fuller realization of what it means to be unique and human. Instead of religious commitment, there were pronouncements, lineal objectives and goals, definitions, rules, all carefully edited and articulated. This group of young novitiates spoke of evil and social injustice, of the importance of using political and economic powers to bring about social changes. They spoke against poverty and war, the end of killing and hunger. But these were devotions to abstractions; for there before us were instances of human suffering, and individuals struggling to rise, and they were being met with indifference, with a refusal or inability to listen and respond. Some spoke glibly of the value of love in worship and in parish work, but these words did not strengthen and affirm, nor support or encourage individuals in their search and struggle. The words were empty. The spirit of life died quickly in the presence of doctrines, rituals, and intellectual reactions. The central concern, the only immediate and intense here-and-now feeling, was a fear of the priests who rated them, an incessant anxiety boardering on paranoia that they were being judged in every detail and nuance. Without exception, the fear of being tossed out, or of being put on probation, was paramount. Some stated they had found a solution to this problem: The way to succeed was to be silent, to speak in abstractions, to avoid action in any living, breathing terms. They were startled at my indignation, at my efforts to arouse genuine caring, interpersonal involvement, and decent human responsiveness. My life with the group of counselors and the group of would-be priests was similar in gross absence of intense, vital, culminating feelings. Each group knew what was required in the professional sense, but both lacked the fullness and depth of a truly human commitment to self and others.

Yes, in both these groups, feelings of intensity and depth were missing, and the love that connects one man with other men never developed because love is immediate and grows out of a willingness to enter into interpersonal dialogue and communication, out of the willingness to permit the unknown in one's self to connect with the unknown in others. Here were people indifferent to human feeling, hour after hour, day by day, people who could talk about the importance of commitment and involvement, who could define and describe responsibility but who were totally unaware of what it means to be within the guts and heart of oneself and within the organic life of others. What had aroused many of the people in these groups to brace themselves against me was my total response, my unequivocal stand, my full reaction to the absence of vivid life, my shocking display of an intensity of feelings.

Nearly all the communications in these groups had been aimed at clarifying past conversations and promoting future understandings and agreements—and these were not even with each other but with people who were not present. What was missing was just what I had been wrestling to recapture myself—a commitment to the unknown, a willingness to discover what must be from unknown sources of life within and without. What was lacking was immediacy, depth, intensity, and a willingness to let go of old biases and to enter uncertainly into a process of rebirth. What was required was an internalization of a value like Thoreau's: "Every part of nature teaches that the passing away of one life is the making room for another."

Because I protested I was regarded as an outsider. In both groups, a battle for truth ensued that kept us awake most of the night. When I considered what had happened, I came to regard the source of my expressions as a mystery. My thoughts and feelings came, not from any attempt to force change, but from an intense and compelling desire to live and to respond fully to life. My communication was a strong and intense response to indifference, to purely self-centered interests, to sleep in the face of tragic searching and suffering. Perhaps these intense feelings were potent enough to break into my own detachment, isolation, and loneliness. In the face of human struggles met with complacency and indifference, I began to feel deeply the tragic nature of the life before me. I began to experience once more an involvement and intoxication with life. The mystery of what it was all about remains to this day. The metaphysical solution I sought never came to me but that did not matter anymore. I was in touch with people again, with all of me, with all of my senses.

I wanted somehow to express in a rush of feeling what I felt they were doing to themselves and each other. My temporary anger took root and moved me forward into each person's struggles, created a stake in the search for communal values.

In both these groups in the midst of upheaval, angry voices and painful awareness, we went off alone to face the night, to enter into the unknown challenge. The spell was broken. It was clear that real life had not been created. Through isolation and solitude perhaps we could pick up the pieces and go on to develop something real. I do not know how it came to be, but in the morning when we met, the first step had been taken. In both groups, there was an awareness that a vital human value was missing—that only if the individual person has a chance to act fully on the life that is within and what it engenders in the way of full and complete expression can new life and new relationships begin to form. To be aware of something was not to *live* it, but it was the essential beginning. It was everything in moving toward this reality.

I have no way to account for the shifts that took place in these groups; I do know how the widespread resistance, opposition, and denial vanished and how it came to be that real people appeared in the dawn of the new day. The concerns and issues of searching individuals became central rather than peripheral, following the long, restless night. While I examined the mystery of this shift, I was reading William James' *The Varieties of Religious Experience.* From a less personal perspective, James had explored the same question and had reached a similar conclusion.

> Neither an outside observer nor the subject who undergoes the process can explain fully how particular experiences are able to change one's center of energy so decisively, or why they so often have to bide their hour to do so. All we know is that there are dead feelings, dead ideas, and cold beliefs, and there are hot and live ones; and when one grows hot and alive within us, everything has to recrystallize about it. . . . And our explanations then get so vague and general that one realizes all the more the intense individuality of the whole phenomenon.

I am content to let the mystery remain. One thing is clear. I returned alive once more, strongly responsive to others, reentering in an interpersonal way with my family, friends, and others. I moved with a heightened vitality and touched what I touched, felt what I felt, heard what I heard. I responded to what cannot be seen with the eyes. My long pilgrimage with the unknown, the expression of hot ideas and live feelings, enabled me to do what I can do and to be who I am. I am willing to let this mystery, this intangible process, this responsiveness to the unknown be the center of my energy now and trust that, in this hot potential, living ideas and living feelings will continue to arise.

References

BAUGHAN, RAYMOND JOHN. *The Sound of Silence.* Boston: United Universalist Assn., 1965.

BESTON, HENRY. *The Outermost House.* New York: Ballantine Books, 1971.

DUMAS, GEORGES. La Tristeese et la Joie, 1900.

JAMES, WILLIAM. *The Varieties of Religious Experience.* New York: Doubleday & Co., Inc., 1902.

LAWRENCE, D. H. *Women In Love.* New York: Bantam Edition, 1969.

MURPHY, MICHAEL. *Golf In The Kingdom.* New York: Viking Books, 1972.